W9-AVK-211

Who On Earth is Sylvia Earle?

Undersea Explorer of the Ocean

Read about other Scientists Saving the Earth

Who on Earth is Aldo Leopold?
Father of Wildlife Ecology
ISBN: 978-1-59845-115-3
ISBN: 1-59845-115-4

Who on Earth is Archie Carr?
Protector of Sea Turtles
ISBN: 978-1-59845-120-7
ISBN: 1-59845-120-0

Who on Earth is Dian Fossey?
Defender of the Mountain Gorillas
ISBN: 978-1-59845-117-7
ISBN: 1-59845-117-0

Who on Earth is Jane Goodall?
Champion for the Chimpanzees
ISBN: 978-1-59845-119-1
ISBN: 1-59845-119-7

Who on Earth is Rachel Carson?
Mother of the Environmental Movement
ISBN: 978-1-59845-116-0
ISBN: 1-59845-116-2

Who On Earth is Sylvia Earle?

Undersea Explorer of the Ocean

Susan E. Reichard

Enslow Publishers, Inc.
40 Industrial Road
Box 398
Berkeley Heights, NJ 07922
USA

http://www.enslow.com

Dedication
To the next generation of ocean lovers:
Abigail, Maxwell, Emily, Alicia, Serena, Ashley.

Library of Congress Cataloging-in-Publication Data

Reichard, Susan E.
  Who on earth is Sylvia Earle? : undersea explorer of the ocean / Susan E. Reichard.
    p. cm. — (Scientists saving the Earth)
  Summary: "Details Sylvia Earle's life, with chapters devoted to her early years, life,
work, writings, and legacy"—Provided by publisher.
  Includes bibliographical references and index.
  ISBN-13: 978-1-59845-118-4 (alk. paper)
  ISBN-10: 1-59845-118-9 (alk. paper)
  1. Earle, Sylvia A., 1935– —Juvenile literature. 2. Underwater exploration—Juvenile
literature. 3. Deep diving—Juvenile literature. 4. Marine biologists—United States—
Juvenile literature. 5. Women marine biologists—United States—Juvenile literature. I. Title.
  QH91.3.E2R45 2009
  551.46092—dc22
  [B]

                                 2008032014

Printed in the United States of America

10 9 8 7 6 5 4 3 2 1

To Our Readers:
We have done our best to make sure all Internet Addresses in this book were active and appropriate
when we went to press. However, the author and the publisher have no control over and assume no
liability for the material available on those Internet sites or on other Web sites they may link to. Any
comments or suggestions can be sent by e-mail to comments@enslow.com or to the address on the
back cover.

♻ Enslow Publishers, Inc., is committed to printing our books on recycled paper. The paper in every
book contains 10% to 30% post-consumer waste (PCW). The cover board on the outside of each book
contains 100% PCW. Our goal is to do our part to help young people and the environment too!

Photo Credits: © Associated Press, p. 88, 93, 101; © boysdean, pp. 6–7; Columbia and "The Silent
World." / Library of Congress, p. 21; © commonwealth.club Photo by William F. Adams, p. 95;
© Connie Bransilver/Photo Researchers, Inc., p. 8; Courtesy of Wildlife Conversation Society, p. 11
(top); © Enslow Publishing Inc., pp. 22 (left), 32; National Oceanic and Atmospheric Administration
(NOAA), pp. 11(bottom), 25, 32, 36–37, 39, 40–41, 46–47, 52, 54, 56, 65, 79, 84, © Robert La
Follett, p. 19; © Robert Ressmeyer/CORBIS, pp. 58–59; 61; © Shutterstock, pp. 42–43, 71, 76–77,
82–83, 94; U.S. Fish and Wildlife, pp. 14–15; United States House of Representatives, p. 99.

Cover Photo: Sylvia Earle prepares to dive in JIM suit in 1970. Credit: National Oceanic and
Atmospheric Administration (NOAA).

Contents

1

Alligator gar

The Urge to Submerge

For twenty blissful minutes, I became one with the river and its residents.

—Sylvia Earle

The water was clear the day when Sylvia Earle took her first dive into the icy water of the Weekiwatchee River in Clearwater, Florida. This was an area that attracted sponge divers. A school friend had borrowed his father's copper diving helmet, compressor, and pump. It was equipment used by her

Dr. Sylvia Earle, holding a crab, is shown diving off the Florida Keys.

friend and his father and had been sitting in their garage.

As Sylvia descended into the water, she was determined to try to become as invisible as she could be, in spite of the noisy flow of bubbles coming from the breathing hose.

As she went deeper into the water, a sharp pain stabbed her ears. Sylvia had to swallow often to stop the pain caused by the increasing water pressure. As she touched down on the bottom of the river, thirty feet below the water's surface, she turned and discovered she was face-to-face with an alligator gar. It watched her curiously before swimming away.

This large fish, known for its alligator-like snout, joined a small group of fish that had gathered around her, no doubt "wondering" what this strange creature was who had invaded their peaceful world.

For twenty wonderful minutes, Sylvia observed the creatures swimming around her. She did not want to leave her newly discovered world, but she began to feel dizzy. She tugged on the air hose to indicate to her friends above that she wanted to come up. Around the same time, a friend decided to dive down to find her. Sylvia did not know at the time that her dizziness was caused by breathing poisonous carbon monoxide gas. She and her friends were horrified to find out later that the air pump was not working properly. Exhaust fumes from the generator were flowing into the air compressor's intake pipe. This was a poisonous mix of carbon dioxide, carbon monoxide, blue smoke, and incombustible fuel. This might have been tragic for Sylvia, but she is not someone who scares easily.

Sylvia always loved the water. When she was three and vacationing with her family at the New Jersey shore, a huge wave knocked her down. But instead of running away, Sylvia went back for more. Her parents were proud of her spunk and fearlessness.

Sylvia's first underwater experience in Clearwater changed her life forever. She knew she had to find a way to be able to explore underwater all the time. She began reading all she could about diving and underwater exploration. She read the works of sea explorers William Beebe and Jacques Cousteau. These men were designing equipment and developing ways to stay underwater for long periods of time. Cousteau promoted a device called an Aqua-Lung. He believed to study fish you must become like a fish.

Her favorite author, William Beebe, wrote articles about the amazing creatures he observed in his underwater chamber called the bathysphere. He viewed beautiful glowing fish with lights down their sides. This made the fish look like ocean liners

In this small craft, Beebe and Otis Barton, the designer of the first bathysphere, were able to dive deeper than anyone had gone before.

Deep under the ocean's surface, it looked as if Beebe and Barton were in an entirely different world. Creatures such as these siphonophores were seen for the first time in the deep ocean.

full of brilliant twinkling lights. Sylvia read his words in an article he wrote: "In this kingdom most of the plants are animals, the fish are friends, the colors are unearthly, . . . miracles become marvels, and marvels recurring wonders."[1]

As an adult, Sylvia Earle remembered William Beebe's story about his first dive in his bathysphere. She had read an article in a magazine in which Beebe explained that exploring the deep and being able to look out of a porthole was very different from looking out of a face mask.

Sylvia wondered how she could obtain a diving helmet and compressor that she could use all the time. She knew she would have to repeat her first diving experience. She had to dive again.

This "urge to submerge," as Sylvia Earle would later call it, would become a lifelong love. A love of the underwater world would shape and mold Earle into one of the world's most important marine scientists and protector of the ocean and its inhabitants.

2

A Scientist Is Born

My parents taught me to leave the world at least as good as I found it.

—Sylvia Earle

Sylvia Earle fell in love with the ocean on her family's annual summer visits to the New Jersey shore. She loved to watch and listen to the waves thunder onto the pale sand of the beach. She liked to watch the creatures too, like the tiny sand crabs that scurried lightly across the sand and the sparkling jellyfish that glided across the water.

She especially loved the horseshoe crabs that washed up on the beach. Sylvia was fascinated by these creatures that would lie still on the sand.

Horseshoe crab

They reminded her of giant ladybugs. They had hard shells like armor and long tails with barbs. Sylvia felt it was her duty to return each and every one she found to the ocean. She would fearlessly pick them up by their spiny tails and gently place them in the surf to return to their watery home.

Earle remembered these creatures fondly in a 1991 interview for the Academy of Achievement. She said:

> I remember the big horse-shoe crabs for example. I thought they were just charming, most people think they're old ugly beasts. Maybe that's part of their charm. They look so strange, but are absolutely harmless. Because of the early opportunities I had to get to know creatures and realize that they really weren't out to bite me or hurt me. If I approached them with gentleness they would respond with gentleness. I found myself, even as a very small child, playing with these big horseshoe crabs, and people coming by and wondering at this little kid fooling around, not hurting them, but just really curious about what made them move. Some of them would seem to get stranded on the beach, and I used to entertain myself by struggling to pick them up, and turn them around and send them back into the sea. Not realizing that they were supposed to come up on the beach and lay their eggs. I thought I was doing a good thing anyway.[1]

Sylvia was born on August 30, 1935. She was the middle child and the only daughter. Her father,

Lewis, was an electrical engineer for the DuPont Corporation. He and his wife, Alice, had moved into an old farmhouse when Sylvia was three years old. Both parents were raised on farms as children, and they enjoyed life on their little farm. They wanted their children to grow up in the country too. Their farmhouse was built in the late 1700s. Lewis Earle was very handy. He worked hard to fix up the house for his family.

Sylvia and her brothers loved living in the country. They liked to explore the creek that ran through their yard. Sylvia also loved the pond filled with interesting creatures. Sylvia's family always had a big garden, and she looked forward to collecting and saving the seeds that they would plant next year.

Her mother loved farm life, especially caring for the animals. Her mother was known as the Bird Lady in their neighborhood. She was known for nursing injured animals back to health. When kids in the neighborhood found an injured bird or animal, they immediately took it to the Bird Lady. Sylvia's mother taught Sylvia and her brothers to respect all living things. She also encouraged her children to notice small details about an animal's beauty and its special place in the world.

With her mother's encouragement, Sylvia began keeping a notebook. She carefully and quietly observed the birds, insects, and animals that lived around her farm. She would spend hours describing these creatures and their habits. She also included drawings of the creatures and their surroundings. Sylvia would bring home frogs and tadpoles to observe for a few days at a time. When her notes were finished, she would return the creatures exactly where she had found them, just as her mother had taught her, Today, Earle thanks her mother for her interest in nature. "I learned from her early in life that if you show respect for other creatures, they won't go out of their way to harm you."[2]

There was no television when Sylvia was a young girl. The Earles had no cows or pigs on their farm, but they did have horses. Riding horses was a favorite activity for Sylvia and her brothers. They often rode the horses in the evening and caught fireflies together. When it was dark or too cold, Sylvia and her brothers spent their evenings playing board games together.

The children loved to draw and read. Sylvia also enjoyed studying her collection of jars where she kept insects, tadpoles, salamanders, and lizards. She loved to read books about animals and adventure stories too. Her family was fortunate to have a set of encyclopedias. Sylvia spent hours reading about plants, animals, and nature. Reading would always play an important part in her life.

When Sylvia Earle was twelve, life began to change for her family. Her younger brother, Evan, had always had a breathing problem, and he became ill more often. He sometimes developed pneumonia. The cold winters of the north were hard for him. His coughing spells were very painful. His mother was kept very busy taking care of him and tending to his special needs.

Around the same time, Lewis Earle became unhappy with his job. The Earles decided to

Boats and ocean in Dunedin, Florida. The Earle family made the move to Dunedin in 1948.

move south to Florida. Lewis would start a new business. The family hoped the warmer climate might also improve Evan's health as well.

In the summer of 1948, the Earle family made the move to Dunedin, Florida. The Earle children loved their New Jersey farm and did not want to leave it. But their disappointment quickly turned to joy when the Earle children saw their new home. The backyard of their new home was now the Gulf of Mexico. The children would not have the woods of their old farm to explore, but, instead, they would have the marshes, dunes, and water of the Gulf of Mexico.

Sylvia continued to turn to books to learn all she could about ocean life. She read about the scientists and explorers who were experts on the ocean and its inhabitants. She continued to study. William Beebe and his books were wonderful treasures for Sylvia. Beebe described what it was like to go underwater in a small submarine-like vehicle. He described small and large ocean creatures that no one else had ever seen.

Sylvia was also inspired by biologist Rachel Carson's best-selling book *The Sea Around Us,* published in 1951. This book would become one of the most important books ever written about the ocean. In the book, Carson tries to explain to readers the importance of the seas and why people need to respect these special waters of the world.

Several years later, Carson wrote an even bigger best seller titled, *Silent Spring*. This book brought further awareness to readers of the growing problems of pollution and pesticides.

Another of Sylvia Earle's favorite underwater explorers, Jacques Cousteau, continued to write about deep-sea adventures in his book *The Silent World*. Cousteau had recently designed and developed a special breathing system for divers. This new system was called SCUBA (Self-Contained Underwater Breathing Apparatus). The crowning piece of his SCUBA was the Aqua-Lung. It allowed divers to stay underwater for much longer periods of time. Sylvia began to imagine herself an explorer and scientist just like her role models, Beebe, Cousteau, and Carson.

It is probably no surprise that Sylvia was an excellent student. She graduated from high school in 1952, when she was

Jacques Cousteau prepares to dive with his Aqua-Lung apparatus.

RACHEL L. CARSON

THE SEA AROUND US

Revised edition w...

⬆ Sylvia Earle was inspired by reading *The Sea Around Us* by Rachel Carson.

Rachel Carson ⬆

still sixteen. That summer, she took a course in marine biology at Florida State University. It would be a summer she would never forget.

Dr. Harold J. Humm was the professor of this class. He believed that the best way to study the ocean and the creatures in it was to actually go there. Sylvia could not contain her excitement. She was finally going to have her opportunity to explore underwater. The chance came when Dr. Humm, several other classmates, and Sylvia went on the ultimate field trip.

The boat anchored five miles out. With simple directions to "breathe naturally" from Dr. Humm, Sylvia gently kicked off from the boat. She now had the opportunity to observe carefully the many details of the underwater world. She loved the feeling of weightlessness as she moved about in the water. She could tumble and somersault gracefully and effortlessly like a dolphin underwater.

Earle recalled her first scuba experience vividly. She was able to swim to a group of sponges, where she found a three-inch-long damsel fish.

She remembered reading about Cousteau's excitement as he described how he loved the freedom and excitement of exploration under the water. Scuba diving allowed him to be like one of the fish in its own world. Scuba allowed him to swim with the sharks. She wanted this for herself as well—not just for a few minutes as a hobby, but for the rest of her life. These thoughts were going through her head when finally there was a tug on the rope, signaling that her time underwater was over. Sylvia wished she had been born with gills.

What would life be like if she were to become a teacher of marine biology like Dr. Humm? Would this be possible? In the 1950s, this was a very unusual job for a woman. Most women were housewives, teachers, or nurses. Earle was determined to enter college and study hard. She would make her dream come true.

That fall, Sylvia Earle entered St. Petersburg Junior College. After earning an associate's degree there, she then transferred to Florida State University. She proved her true dedication to marine science by her hard work and passion. She received her bachelor of science (BS) degree from Florida State University in 1955.

After Earle graduated, she learned that Dr. Humm had decided to take a teaching position at Duke University in North Carolina. Earle wanted to continue to learn from her mentor, and she decided to enroll at Duke so she could begin studying for her master's (MA) and doctorate (PhD) degrees. She made a commitment to study botany, the study of plant life.

Earle had been observing and taking notes on plants since her days as a child on the family farm in New Jersey. She continued this interest at her home

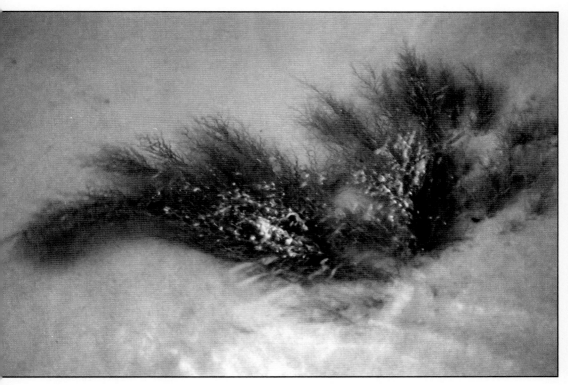

⬆ Marine algae in the shallow waters off the Gulf of Mexico. Earle decided she would devote her studies at Duke University to the study of marine algae.

in Florida, where she also observed the creatures and plants of the salt marshes.

Earle decided she would devote her studies at Duke to small plants called algae. She wanted to become a scientist. Her mentor, Dr. Humm, was her inspiration. His love of the study of ocean plants, especially algae, influenced Earle's desire to study these tiny plants and learn all she could about them and their importance to the ocean's ecosystem.

Her decision to study algae might seem an unusual choice. Earle believed that algae were more than just green scum that floated on top of the water. Some people even called them stinky seaweed. Earle knew that without algae the world would not be as it is today. She knew that all life depends on this single-celled miracle plant.

Over the next few years, Earle would dive, draw, and catalogue the specimens she collected. She observed where the plants were found and what creatures lived around the plants or lived to eat them. She measured the water conditions where the plants lived. She recorded other infor-mation, such as the currents, temperature of the water, the depth, the presence of light, and the amount of salt found in the water. Earle also drew detailed pictures of her samples. She became a very skilled artist. To preserve her plant speci-mens, she pressed and dried them. Her collection of samples is a large and impressive contribution to the study of marine science.

Earle's education and dedication to her work kept her busy for many years. In 1957, she fell in love and married John Taylor. Taylor was also a student at Duke and was studying to be a zoologist. Earle was twenty-one years old. She and her husband decided to move to Florida. In 1960, their daughter, Elizabeth, was born. Two years later, a son, John Ritchie, was born.

Earle worked very hard to balance her life as a wife, mother, scientist, and student. She was determined not to allow anything to keep her from her goals: "I could no more imagine not being a scientist, than not having a backbone."[3]

Earle decided to focus her research on algae. Although this marine plant seems like an unusual choice, Earle knew that algae provides homes, protection, and food for many ocean creatures. Algae have been known to even inspire poets and songwriters. She realized that these tiny plants must surely have almost magical elements.

Scientists know that life everywhere began with plants. This made Earle feel sure that her decision to focus her research on algae was a good one. To Earle, these tiny plants were more than just slimy seaweed or green scum. She hoped that her research would benefit science. Not only would her topic be a unique one to research and write about, but the fact that she was a woman in a male-dominated field would also make her work unique.

An unusual and exciting opportunity for research came Earle's way in 1962. A research ship, *Anton Brunn,* needed one more scientist for an important expedition sponsored by the National Science Foundation. Dr. Humm, who was involved with the project, suggested Earle for this position. The scientists would be traveling and completing their research in the world's largest bodies of water. Earle's parents offered to help her husband with the children, cooking, and taking care of the house for the six-week trip. It would be hard for Earle to leave her young children for such a long time, but the scientist in her knew she could not pass up this once-in-a-lifetime opportunity.

Not everyone was pleased that Earle would be part of the research expedition. Some of these scientists and researchers actually believed that a woman onboard a ship would bring bad luck. Earle thought this notion was ridiculous. She also thought it was silly when a newspaper reporter asked her if her husband minded that she was the only woman among the seventy researchers.

From the moment she arrived on board the *Anton Brunn,* Earle knew she would have to prove herself to the men. She worked very hard and got very little sleep. She would wake up at 5:00 AM to go diving and mind her own business and stay out of everyone's way. Earle did not intrude on their parties and ignored their jokes. She discovered that if she worked twice as hard and kept her sense of humor, everything would work out.

Earle loved her early morning dives off the ship. On one dive, Earle was joined by several fish specialists. As they went deeper and deeper, she noticed a strange bright pink plant. She knew almost immediately from her experiences that this was not a plant, she had seen before. As the dive team moved closer to the pink plant, they discovered a tiny forest of bright pink plants. Earle would describe this unknown plant as looking like palm trees that had been turned inside out. She had the great privilege of naming this newly discovered plant because she had been the first to see it. She named this new species the *Humbrella hydra*. The name would remind people of its shape, and it honored her teacher and mentor, Dr. Humm. During the next two years, Earle would take part in four more research expeditions on the *Anton Brunn*.

The next year was a period of mixed emotions for Earle. She proudly received her PhD from Duke University. Her research work on brown algae was an important contribution to science. Sadly, her nine-year marriage to John Taylor ended in divorce.

Earle was not a person who sat around dwelling on negative circumstances. She was eager to move on to her next diving project. In the meantime, she fell in love, and in 1966, she married Giles Mead. Dr. Mead was the curator of fish at Harvard University's Museum of Comparative Zoology. The couple had met while working on research expeditions together. Their Boston household was a busy blended family of five children, and, before too long, Earle was expecting her third child.

One day, while Mead was at work at the museum, he saw an announcement from the Smithsonian Institution in Washington, D.C., on a bulletin board. Mead would tell his wife about the notice, and it would soon change Sylvia Earle's life.

3

"Her Deepness"

Tektite lifted me from the realm of pure science to communicating with a broad audience. Suddenly there were microphones in front of me and millions of people were hearing what I had to say. I felt a strong obligation to help educate them about the oceans.

—Sylvia Earle

In 1969, the U.S. government began a new program that would allow scientists to live and work under the sea. This would take place in the U.S. Virgin Islands. The program was called Tektite, named for the pieces of green glass from space that are found in the sea.[1] Four men were to stay

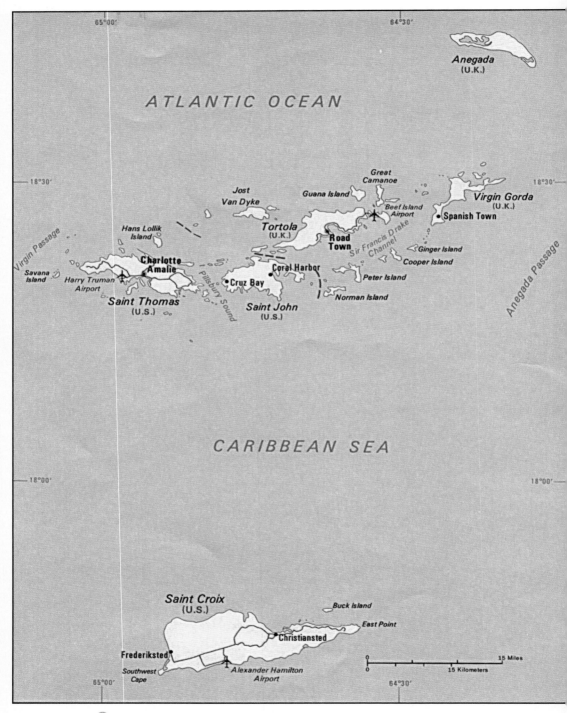

The U.S. Virgin Islands.

submerged for two full months. They would live, study, and complete their research in a four-room building. Cables from the undersea habitat ran to a shore-based system that provided the air, water, and power for the men. *(The Tektite Habitat was an underwater laboratory was the home to divers during Tektite I and II programs. Tektite was the first scientists-in-the-sea program sponsored nationally. The habitat capsule was placed in Great Lameshur Bay, Saint John, U.S. Virgin Islands, in 1969 and again in 1970.)*

Sylvia Earle's husband, Dr. Giles Mead, discovered this announcement on a bulletin board at the museum where he worked. The advertisement informed scientists and engineers that the second part of this program was about to begin. The program was in need of fifty scientists and engineers for a two-week stay in the Tektite habitat.[2]

Earle could not believe it: "Two weeks! Not just in and out for half an hour or so at a time, three or four times a day, but all day every day and all night. Underwater for *fourteen* days straight! What a concept!"[3]

Earle was very surprised and dismayed to discover that no women were expected to apply for this opportunity to live in the Tektite habitat. Earle called the people in charge of the project and was amazed when they asked her to lead an entire team of women. Earle had more diving experience,

A model of the Tektite Habitat. It was placed in Great Lameshur Bay, St. John, Virgin Islands, in 1969 and again in 1970. The underwater laboratory was the home to divers during Tektite I and II programs.

more than one thousand hours, than other women. Her impressive résumé and her diving experience made her the natural choice to lead this team. Earle decided this was not an experience she could ignore. Her parents generously volunteered to take care of her children during her adventure. Her children were excited that their mother had this unusual opportunity. Earle gave up her teaching and research responsibilities at Harvard University for a time to participate in this exciting endeavor.

The United States Department of the Interior coordinated Tektite II, with part of the funding coming from NASA, which was interested in the psychological study of the scientific teams working in closed environments, similar to that of spacecraft.

The missions were carried out in 1970. The Tektite II comprised ten missions lasting ten to twenty days with four scientists and an engineer on each mission.

The all-women's aquanaut team led by Earle was named Mission 6. The other scientists participating in the all-female mission included Renate True of Tulane, as well as Ann Hartline and Alina Szmant, graduate students at Scripps Institute of Oceanography. The fifth member of the crew was Margaret Ann Lucas, a Villanova engineering graduate, who served as Habitat Engineer. Each

The first all woman team-in-training for the Tektite II program in 1970.

woman would have her own projects to complete during their two-week stay in the Tektite habitat. The Tektite II missions were the first to undertake in-depth ecological studies.

Almost overnight, Earle became a media sensation. The newspaper headlines read: "Beacon Hill Housewife to Lead Team of Female Aquanauts." Earle was disappointed that after a decade of hard work, she was thought of as a housewife first and a scientist second. But this was the mistaken thinking of these times. She was not a person to dwell on the negative headlines. Earle focused on preparing mentally and physically for her underwater adventure.

Earle discovered that many television and radio reporters would be following the Tektite women and their undersea adventure for their readers and listeners. Earle knew she must use this opportunity to let people know about the ocean and how it was rapidly changing, and not for the better. What an opportunity for Earle and the other scientists! People could now actually see what the scientists were seeing underwater. She knew that people would then be motivated to take care of the ocean. Earle believed the public would never know about these issues if no one told them.

The Tektite underwater habitat was unusual looking. It was a large rectangular base that supported two cylinder-shaped structures. Each

The Tektite II team, lead by Sylvia Earle (far right), participate in rebreather training.

The Tektite II team relaxes in crew quarters, including Sylvia Earle in a black-and-white suit.

cylinder contained two chambers that were stacked on top of each other. There was a flexible tunnel that connected the two chambers. There were four rooms, like an underwater motel. There was a laboratory that was full of equipment. There was a social area with carpeting and television. There was also a full kitchen area that included a freezer full of frozen food and yogurt. In addition there was also a sleeping area. The scientists spent as much time as they could outside in the water, because they might never have another opportunity like this again.

Earle was so excited about being able to observe underwater for such long periods of time. The new breathing system allowed the women to rebreathe their own air after it was purified in the air pack they wore on their backs. The breathing system also had the advantage of being very quiet and allowed them to observe underwater almost unnoticed by the inhabitants.

Earle's duties during the Tektite project were to survey plant species that grew in the reef areas, and she wanted to learn how algae were affected by the grazing fish. Earle hoped to show that the presence of the scientists would not have an impact on the life on the coral reef.

Earle stated in her book *Sea Change: A Message From the Oceans:*

One of the great joys of being a dweller on a reef is the ease of being up and about early, while it is still full dark, slipping into quiet water, and gliding without lights to the reef's edge where many dawn risers tend to congregate. Five gray angelfish were among the first to emerge from their nighttime crevices and every morning, same time, same place, begin their slow waltz around the mounds of coral, pausing now and then to nibble a bit of sponge or nose at a lump of algal debris. There were also several species of parrotfish, all fitted with fused chompers that much resemble the bill of the birds for which they are named. As colorful as macaws, the parrotfish, like many birds, are active by day and sleep at night, but unlike any parrot or other bird I have ever heard about, these extraordinary fish often spin a clear gelatinous cocoon around themselves and slumber in a trance-like state robed in goo.[4]

Within two weeks, Earle observed day and night behavior of thirty-six kinds of plant-eating fish in fourteen families and 145 different kinds of plants, including twenty-six species never found before in the Virgin Islands.

At the end of the two weeks, the women were greeted with roses and were given a ticker-tape parade in downtown Chicago. Everywhere they went, they were treated like rock stars. The women received medals for their accomplishment from the Conservation Service. Earle and the other women on the team found themselves facing

Rusty parrotfish

dozens of microphones, with millions of people waiting to hear what they had to say. Earle could only think of her beloved ocean. She knew she had to take this opportunity to reach as many people as she could with her message. She knew she had to let people know about the irreversible damage they were causing to the ocean. People had to know that if the ocean was damaged, we would all be damaged.

Earle was changed forever by her two-week underwater stay in the Tektite habitat. She wished everyone could have the opportunity to live underwater for just one day. People's ignorance of the ocean was its greatest threat. The 1970s were an exciting time for exploration and discovery both in space and underwater. The first men landed and walked on the moon in July 1969. There was renewed interest in our world. The very first Earth Day was established by Congress in 1970. The first National Marine Sanctuary would be set up in 1975. This sanctuary would be a protected underwater park where plants and animals are protected from harm. Earle hoped all this interest in our planet Earth would also include interest in the largest part of our world, the oceans.

Earle was thrilled to receive many invitations to speak publicly about her discoveries and experiences underwater. She wrote many articles that appeared in national magazines. Millions read these magazines and would read Earle's message to the people about the ocean. She wanted ordinary people to understand how important this large and mostly unexplored world is that lay beneath the surface of the water.

Earle's professional life was very exciting, and she continued to receive many speaking engagements. However, she was very sad that her second marriage to Dr. Giles Mead ended in divorce. She and her children left the East Coast to make their new home in Oakland, California.

Earle had spent most of her education and career studying the tiniest of plants in the ocean. Putting the past behind her in 1977, she decided to spend a year studying the largest of creatures, the humpback whale.

Earle and underwater photographer Al Giddings would be working with Roger and Katy Payne, two scientists who were studying whales and their songs. The Paynes, along with Earle and Giddings, were also filming a documentary film for *National Geographic*. For three months, the foursome would follow the whales. Giddings was the first person to ever photograph humpbacks singing.

Earle and Giddings dove into the clear water of the Pacific Ocean off the coast of Hawaii to study and photograph the humpback whales for

Peggy Lucas, inside Tektite, observes diver Sylvia Earle.

National Geographic. After just a few seconds in the water, Earle observed a huge black form hurtling toward her like a locomotive. Although a collision with the small scientist seemed a sure thing, the gentle giant slid past Earle, giving her what seemed to be a look of curiosity. Earle's fear of the humpbacks left her immediately after that encounter, and she discovered a new friend.

Humpbacks usually grow to be forty feet long and can weigh as much as forty tons. They are known to be gentle creatures. In earlier times, whales had been hunted for meat and oil. They had been hunted almost to the point of extinction. Fortunately, new laws stopped most of this slaughter.

Earle wanted to study the whales and learn their role in the ecology of the oceans. She thought of the whales as floating islands in the sea, because "like a ships hull, the whale's hide is a home for a variety of barnacles, algae, and parasites."[5] Most scientific information known about whales has been gathered from dead whales. Earle studied these amazing creatures in their own world.

Earle and Giddings were concerned that their presence in the water would disturb the whales. As the pair carried out their research and photo taking, they discovered the whales were as curious about them as they were about the whales:

Whales are like swallows, they are like otters. They are in a three-dimensional world, and they move in any direction. They swim upside down. They're vertical. They're every which way. Sometimes they are horizontal, but not always. Once in a while they are horizontal. And they are so supple! Many of the renderings of whales that you see in books make them look big and fat and ponderous and lumpy. They are sleek and elegant and gorgeous, among the most exquisite creatures on the planet. They move like ballerinas.[6]

Once during a dive with the whales, Earle was so focused on whale watching that she did not notice the large white-tipped shark that was almost touching her flippers. She kicked at the shark; it darted away, circled Earle once, and came back at her. She kicked again and noticed a second shark moving in toward her. Then, as mysteriously as they had appeared, they were gone. Earle thought that perhaps the sharks had not found her very appetizing.

Earle's year with the whales was a magical one, but she feared for the creatures. The film *Gentle Giants of the Pacific* shows Earle swimming gracefully around the whales. Earle shared her love of whales with the world. She visited more than twenty countries and showed the movie and spoke about her adventures. Earle made people aware of the importance of these great creatures in our world. Swimming with them is something Earle will never forget.

⬆ Underwater shot of humpback whale.

Shortly after their adventure with the whales, Giddings had another idea. He wanted Earle to take a walk on the bottom of the ocean. They both believed it was important for people to actually see what the floor of the ocean looked like. People would then better understand the importance of deep-sea exploring. Giddings and Earle would create this adventure for a *National Geographic* television special.

Earle had heard about a special diving suit called the Jim suit. It was named for the first person to wear the suit, diver Jim Jarrett. It had been worn by people who had to make underwater repairs to ships and bridges and oil rigs in the ocean.

Earle could not turn down Giddings's idea. Earle was about to have the book she and Giddings had worked on published by *National Geographic*. The book would be a full-color book on the history of underwater exploration. Titled *Exploring the Deep,* the book was published in 1980 and opened up the ocean world to its many readers. She would use the fame this dive would bring to once again draw the world's attention to the bottom of the sea. Earle would be the first scientist to use the Jim suit. Although there were great dangers involved in this dive, Giddings and Earle raised the money and received funding from *National Geographic* as well. They also had to round up a team of scientists to help. Some of the scientists

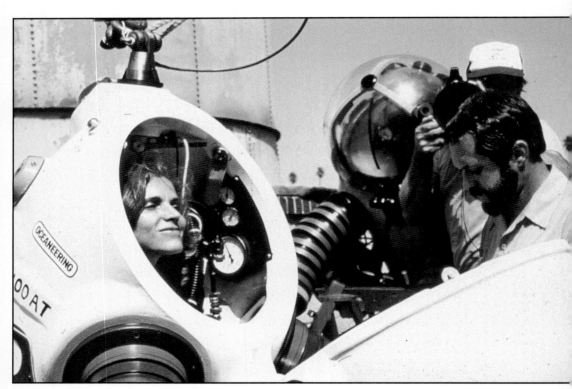

🔼 Dr. Sylvia Earle prepares to dive in a JIM suit in 1970.

were very worried about the dangers involved, but Earle was ready for this new adventure.

Once she was in the Jim suit, Earle would be taken down to the ocean floor by a small under-water vehicle called a submersible. She would be attached to it by a thin cord. With this method, Earle could go down as far as fifteen hundred feet, where she could then explore. She would be unhooked from the cord to walk about on the ocean floor. No one had ever walked on the floor of the ocean before.

The Jim suit resembles a space suit. The suit is made of very tough material, because it must be able to withstand the great water pressure found at these depths. The suit has thick but flexible arms that are almost accordion-like. The arms have large, round elbows. The wrist joints end with steel grippers that are used for the hands and fingers. Earle practiced in the Jim suit for many hours in a large tank of water. She said she felt like a walking refrigerator in the bulky suit. She even needed to add weights to her feet to hold her down in the water, as she weighed only 110 pounds. Giddings and the scientists on the team could not stop thinking about the many things that could possibly go wrong with this dive. What if the line broke between the Jim suit and the submersible? What if the suit leaked? Would the pressure harm Earle? What if the ship waiting for them on the

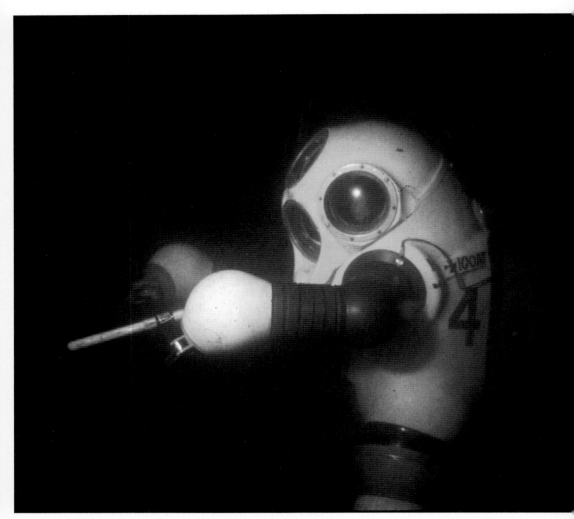

⬦ Aquanaut underwater in a JIM suit.

surface of the water lost track of them? Earle could not spend her time worrying about these possibilities. She was ready to explore.

The tiny yellow vehicle that would take Earle on her dive went below on October 19, 1979, off the coast of Hawaii. Earle was so excited. She watched as the water gradually changed color the deeper she went. It started out light blue and darkened to an almost deep purple color. Earle wanted to go as deep as possible. At 1,250 feet, though, the little submersible stopped. The seascape Earle observed was remarkable. Shrimp and coral, with tiny lights that glowed in the dark, were all around her. Then the final moment came, the moment when Earle was released from the line and the submersible. Earle was free. Jellyfish drifted by her along with seven-foot-long rays. Scores of fish and even a small shark swam by. Earle was recording everything she saw in her notebook. She would later write for National Geographic, "It was like walking on a moonless night."[7] While she explored, the tiny submersible followed behind her.

Two and one-half hours later, Giddings's voice told Earle that the time was up. She could not believe it. It was as if only twenty minutes had passed. Before she left the ocean floor, Earle planted two flags: the flag of the United States and a flag representing the National Geographic Society. This was to mark the historic event in

Deep-sea diver and marine biologist Sylvia Earle and engineer Graham Hawkes, the husband-and-wife team behind Deep Ocean Engineering, examine a model of the company's latest project, the two-person submersible *Mantis*.

ocean exploration. No other person had walked on the ocean floor at that depth.

When Earle arrived home after her history-making dive, her children greeted her. They led her to the kitchen, where they had proudly displayed on the refrigerator door the headline story from the tabloid newspaper *The Star.* The headline read: "Brave mom's historic dive to the bottom of the world."[8] Earle was glad people were learning about deep-ocean exploration. As a scientist, however, she was not sure she wanted to be in the same newspaper that was known for stories about giant man-eating insects and green men from Mars.

Earle was very proud of her most recent accomplishment. She had earned the unique title of "Her Deepness" from the press and her peers. She was still frustrated, however, by the government's lack of interest and funding for the ocean. The earth is 70 percent water. Earle believed people wanted and needed to understand how all life depends on the ocean. Surprisingly, only 1 percent of the world has been explored underwater.

Sylvia Earle and Graham Hawkes, who she had recently married, decided to start a business together to make underwater vehicles for deep-ocean exploration. They called their businesses Deep Ocean Technology and Deep Ocean Engineering.

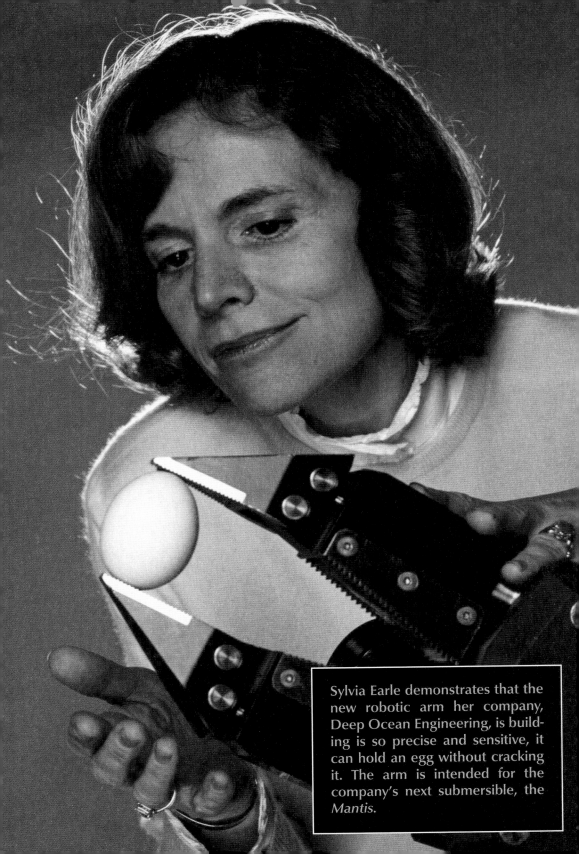

Sylvia Earle demonstrates that the new robotic arm her company, Deep Ocean Engineering, is building is so precise and sensitive, it can hold an egg without cracking it. The arm is intended for the company's next submersible, the *Mantis*.

Earle did not enjoy the business world and had trouble selling their vehicles, also known as ROVs (remotely operated vehicles). They were expensive, and exploring was expensive. Finally, one of their Deep Rover submersibles was purchased by Shell Oil. This vehicle was made of clear plastic and looked like a small bubble. With Deep Rover, Earle set another record for deep solo diving—three thousand feet. She recalled the hundreds of dolphins swimming around her. She also remarked that diving in the deep ocean was like falling into a galaxy of little stars or the Fourth of July fireworks. Even though the ocean is dark at deep depths, the bioluminescence, or light from the creatures that live there, provides an experience like no other.

The following year, Hawkes designed a smaller and lighter submersible called Phantom. Customers in more than thirty countries bought these underwater vehicles for many types of jobs. Some of these jobs were fixing underwater oil rigs and military tasks that required underwater vehicles. The vehicle was also used by police to search underwater crime scenes. Even Disney World bought a Phantom to show visitors what life would be like in the ocean. It was part of their Living Seas Pavilion. Visitors saw what they might look like from the point of view of the creatures living in the ocean.

Earle left her position at Deep Ocean Engineering to take a very important job as chief scientist for the National Oceanic and Atmospheric Administration (NOAA). Earle was honored that President H. W. Bush appointed her to be the first woman ever to have this job.

Earle's reputation as a scientist and ocean advocate was growing. She held diving records and had spent more than six thousand hours underwater. Other scientists honored Earle by naming species found after her. Some of these include *Diadema sylvie,* a small sea urchin, and a red alga they named *Pilinia earleae.* Unfortunately, her marriage to her third husband, Graham Hawkes, was ending. Earle always tried her best to juggle her private and professional life, but she always seemed to choose her life as a scientist.

Earle's children were grown, and she left her home in California to move to Washington, D.C. She was fifty-five years old and eager to begin her new job. Her appointment as chief scientist kept her very busy. She had to attend many meetings and speak before Congress, but Earle still made time for exploring.

In 1991, the Japanese government invited her to go on a research dive in a three-person submersible. The little vessel named *Shinkai 6500* took Earle thirteen thousand feet down, farther down in the ocean than she had ever been.

Earle planned to use her new position as chief scientist at NOAA to persuade the U.S. government to invest money in underwater research. She was disappointed to learn that no one was interested in underwater research. After time, in frustration, Earle left her position at NOAA.

Before she left her job, however, Earle still had one important job to complete. Once before, Earle had investigated oil spills. That disaster in March 1989 had changed her thinking. Over 11 million gallons of crude oil had escaped from an oil tanker, the *Exxon Valdez,* near the Alaskan shore. It caused environmental damage that was almost beyond repair. Earle realized that human behavior was hurting and destroying her beloved ocean and its inhabitants. No one could imagine what the long-term effects would be on this beautiful shoreline in Alaska.

This time the oil spill was caused by war. In 1991, Saddam Hussein, the Iraqi dictator, invaded Kuwait, his neighbor to the south. He had wanted his army to capture Kuwait's rich oil fields. American troops were sent over to launch Operation Desert Storm. The Iraqi soldiers retreated back to their own country. In revenge, the Iraqi soldiers set fire to eight hundred oil wells and dumped more than 12 million barrels of oil on Kuwait soil and the beautiful Persian Gulf. Earle was sent to investigate.

⬆ Wild ducks killed as a result of the *Exxon Valdez* oil spill in 1989. Thousands of animals died immediately after the oil spill. The best estimates are: 250,000 to as many 500,000 seabirds, at least 1,000 sea otters, 300 harbor seals, 250 bald eagles, as well as the destruction of billions of salmon and herring eggs.

When she arrived, she looked out and saw the beaches clogged with oil. Earle was afraid that no one would be aware of the impact that the oil spill would have on the environment. Earle wanted the world to know about the damage that had been done. She held a press conference to tell people that much of the wildlife had been killed and the environmental damage was worse than anyone had thought.

Dr. Earle was glad to once again be a private citizen, because she could now freely speak her mind and not be a representative of the administration in office. She could tell others about the importance of a healthy ocean. Earle felt responsible for the world's oceans. In addition to the oil spills, there were other reasons for worry. Cruise ships and airplanes regularly discarded their trash and waste into the oceans. Chemicals from farming and industry were poisoning the rivers and streams that lead to the oceans.

Earle saw other problems in the world's oceans, and these issues caused her concern as well. The dumping of trash and the rising ocean temperatures from global warming were bleaching and smothering the coral reefs of the world. Fishing nets, some more than forty feet long, were destroying creatures and their habitats. Even Earle's beloved childhood backyard of the Gulf of Mexico was becoming polluted. Earle never started out to become an environmentalist. She began to think she could make more of a difference as a private citizen than as a deep-sea diver. She wanted to actively seek and not just talk about the need for healthy oceans. Earle would spend more time on land so she could spread her ocean message.

Earle now could spend all her time informing others about the importance of caring for the oceans. She appeared on many television shows, including *Mr. Roger's Neighborhood*. Many films were made about the work she had done. She spoke in more than sixty countries around the world about the oceans, its creatures, and their problems.

Earle decided to write a book about her many diving experiences and the danger of not caring for the oceans. Her book, *Sea Change: A Message of the Oceans* was published in 1995. Readers learned how critical the ocean is to our survival as human beings.

4

Oceans of Trouble

The ocean is our life support system. . . . [I]f we want to take care of ourselves, we need to start by taking care of the ocean.

—*Sylvia Earle*

Sylvia Earle's popularity with the public gave her the perfect platform as a private citizen to inform people of the many problems causing trouble for the ocean. Earle believes the ocean is the world's bank, where many of our earth's priceless resources are stored. "Trash is clogging the arteries of the planet," she told an audience in a speech she delivered at the World Bank in Washington in 2007.[1]

Plastics, which are very important to our lives, are also hard to dispose of safely. Much of this plastic ends up in the ocean. Such items as straws, plastic drink bottles, toys, bags, and many other items end up choking wildlife when accidentally swallowed. Fishing nets and fishing gear also end up in the ocean and snare and entangle the sea creatures as well as birds.

Pollution is not the only problem that is destroying the oceans. People are the greatest predators of the creatures of the sea. All over the world, the appetite for fish is causing a decline in many species. Fish is the most widely traded item in the world today. More than 90 million tons of fish are taken every year from the ocean. Some modern fishing techniques use thousands of miles of drift nets to drag the sea floor and scoop up everything in their path. Many of these nets are illegal today, but even the nets that are now allowed snare sea turtles, dolphins, whales, sharks, and other unintended fish.

Earle has made a life decision not to eat fish anymore herself. Cod, snapper, grouper, swordfish, halibut, sharks, tuna, shrimp, blue crabs, and oysters are all on the list of ocean wildlife whose numbers are declining. Earle states, "In just a few decades almost 90% of the ocean's large fish have been almost eliminated."[2]

Many of the fish consumed also contain high levels of mercury, pesticides, and raw sewage. This fish may or may not be safe to eat. In an interview with Alison Caldwell of *The World Today,* Earle reports that "it is the high-end luxury market for fish that is consuming much of the fish that are taken. These fish are not feeding millions of starving people. There are over 1 billion people who rely on fish as their main source of food. In some places, local fisherman cannot catch enough fish to feed their villages."[3]

Earle also has great concerns for coral reefs. She knows that these busy underwater cities of the ocean are in great trouble. She wants people to understand that the reefs are a reflection of the health of the ocean. The ocean's trouble soon may become people's trouble.

Global warming is raising the temperature of the oceans. Coral reefs cannot survive at these high temperatures. These warmer waters kill the algae that feed the reef. This process is called coral bleaching.

Coral reefs provide shelter for thousands of sea creatures, including some so tiny they can only be seen under a microscope. Reefs are also called the underwater rain forests because so many different species live there. One of every four ocean creatures lives on coral reefs.

Coral reef

According to Earle, half the coral reefs are already gone. She also believes the good news is that half the reefs are still in good shape, so there is a chance to save them. In addition to global warming, other factors hurting coral reefs are all caused by humans. Some of these factors include pollution, overfishing with huge drift nets, and building projects along shorelines.

Coral reefs are an important part of the world's ecosystem. Not only do they help keep nature in balance in the ocean, but parts of coral reefs and the creatures that live among them provide medicines that can be used for asthma, heart disease, leukemia, and viruses.[4]

In an interview with television correspondent Betty Ann Bowser, Earle explained that coral reefs were starting to be protected areas under the Marine Sanctuary program. The eighteen thousand square miles of U.S. coral reefs are under this protection now. Of course, there are coral reefs all over the world, and that fact makes protecting reefs a global concern.

In 2005, Earle began an expedition to use deep exploration minisub vehicles to study the Pulley Ridge coral reef. This is America's deepest reef which had been discovered during the Sustainable Seas Expeditions—a five-year project to explore the underwater marine world. Scientists were amazed to find this deep reef was full of healthy corals and sea life. Earle and other scientists wanted to discover what it was that made this deep coral reef so healthy while other more shallow reefs around the world were dying. The scientists took many small samples from the reef and discovered microscopic bacteria that glowed in the dark. These samples are still being studied today. Perhaps their discoveries will help coral reefs that are dying today.

In addition to studying natural reefs, Earle's scientific work also included exploring artificial reefs. These reefs are created from sunken ships, such as warships, that have been sent to the bottom of the sea. Over time, these artificial reefs resemble natural reefs and provide scientists with valuable information. Sylvia Earle and *National Geographic* photographer Al Giddings made more than two hundred dives in 1975. One of these artificial reefs is called Truk Lagoon and lies off the Caroline Islands in the western Pacific Ocean. Earle and Giddings dove into the crystal blue waters to study the growth times of coral and the abundant sea life living in and around the lagoon. More than sixty war ships lay on the sea bottom in this region and provided the skeleton for the artificial reef. This gave the reef a good start to take hold and grow.

No one had ever recorded the varieties of plants and animals that settled and grew on these artificial reefs. It was Earle's goal to document more than thirty years of life on the reef. She started by recording and tagging the size of the largest corals, then worked down to the smallest. She would return to the same spot at a later time to see how much these specimens had grown.

Earle recorded the different species of fish that lived in the artificial reef. One of these was a beautiful lionfish that had made its home in one of the gun turrets on a sunken battleship. Earle very carefully tried to encourage the fish to come out and have its picture taken by Giddings. The lionfish did not budge from its home. Earle recalls what happens next in an article in *National Geographic:*

> Inching forward, I eased my hand along the fish's tail. It responded to my gentle motion and began moving into the open. Then it did something I had not anticipated: It made an abrupt tilt in my direction with its dorsal spines, a defensive motion. I waited a moment before moving again, but the fish was evidently alarmed, for it tilted again. That was enough for me. I started to withdraw my hand, but the lionfish suddenly tilted once more, this time vigorously, and through my diving glove I felt a sharp jab below the nail of one finger . . . Removing my glove, I examined my finger and saw a trickle of green blood—as it appears more than 50 feet below the surface. I was in trouble and I knew it.[5]

Because it was their second dive of the day, Earle and Giddings required an hour's decompression before they reached the surface to avoid the bends. This is a very painful and often fatal condition that occurs from the water pressure caused by the formation of nitrogen bubbles in the bloodstream. As the pain began to spread through her hand, Earle says, "[I] closed my eyes and could think of nothing but the intense, stabbing agony that was building in my finger. . . . After 45 minutes my finger had swelled to nearly double its normal size and my arm and shoulder began to ache as well . . . the burning in my finger continued for two more hours."[6] Giddings helped her board the boat, and although the worst was over, her finger was tender and swollen for days. On this particular dive into the reef, Earle discovered a new species of red alga and fifteen unknown species that were growing in this area of the Pacific. She observed and recorded hundreds of parrotfish, blennies, groupers, snappers, and barracudas. From the tiniest of egg sacs observed to the larger predator fish, a giant tuna found on the reef, all have their special roles that are important to the reef's health and the health of the whole ocean.

Earle's concerns about ocean health also includes the humpback whales. Until the 1970s, no one had tried to study the whales where they lived.

Lionfish

Earle's opportunity came in 1977 with scientists Katy and Roger Payne.

Almost all the earth's nine great whale species had been hunted to the point of extinction by commercial whaling methods. Scientists knew a lot about dead whales, but they did not know much about how they lived until Earle and the Paynes studied them. Strange items had been found inside the stomachs of dead whales, including rubber boots, license plates, plastic toys, rocks, coconuts, and whole fishing nets. By the 1930s, more than fifty thousand whales were killed every year. No longer were they killed by hand with harpoons or long spears. Now they were killed by huge factory ships. The whales would be used for cosmetics, oil, and food for animals. Today, most whale hunting has been banned, but many whales are still on the endangered list. Now, humpbacks are fully protected by the International Whaling Commission.

Earle studied how whale mothers tended to their babies. She noticed that they stayed together and even slept together. Earle and the other scientists followed the whales from Hawaii to their summer feeding grounds in the Aleutian Islands off the coast of Alaska. Her observations and Giddings's photography showed these gentle giants of the Pacific to the world in their documentary film.

A mother and baby humpback whale.

In *Dive,* her book for young readers, Earle writes:

> [P]eople all over the world now recognize the importance of whales for something more than a meal and most nations have stopped killing them. Some engineers even use whales as design models for submarines and other equipment that moves underwater. Scientists are also learning how whales communicate and navigate over thousands of miles without maps. These creatures are impossible to replace once they are gone.[7]

Today, thanks to Earle's and other scientists' work, the National Marine Sanctuary use hundreds of volunteers at shore sites in and around Hawaii to count humpback whales and record their behavior.

Overfishing also causes harm to the creatures that get caught along with the fish intended for the catch. Earle and other scientists have asked governments not to allow the fishing methods that harm the Pacific leatherback sea turtles. They, along with all sea turtles, are endangered by these modern fishing methods. These ancient creatures were swimming the seas when dinosaurs still lived and roamed the earth. The leatherback sea turtles are the only ones without shells. The sea turtle population has decreased from ninety-one thousand to less than three thousand in a little more than twenty years. Earle believes that the decline in the last five years is nothing short of catastrophic.

These amazing creatures are among the earth's most ancient creatures and are also among the largest reptiles. They can grow more than nine feet long and weigh more than two thousand pounds. They are just one of six types of sea turtles that are endangered. The hawksbill and Kemp's ridley, along with the leatherback are listed as endangered. The breeding population of Olive Ridley and green sea turtles are endangered along Mexico's Pacific Coast, and threatened elsewhere.

Thanks to Earle and others, some measures are now being taken to save the leatherback turtles. In 2004, Earle took part in a film, *Last Journey for the Leatherback?* This documentary demonstrates the threat to the turtles by industrial fishing methods. In the film, Earle explains that sea turtles are really symbolic of what is happening to the oceans as a whole. As the sea turtles go, so goes the ocean. The film sounds the alarm about the threat of extinction to sea turtles worldwide. Earle says, "Sea turtles have been called the ocean's 'canary in the coal mine,' for they warn us of threats to the health of our oceans."[8]

Leatherbacks are often caught up in fishing nets. Sometimes they also mistake plastic debris in the ocean for jellyfish. They eat the plastic. This makes them feel full so they do not eat. They are

Sea turtle

Before turtle excluder devices (TED), many loggerhead turtles were casualties of shrimping operations.

hungry, but they starve to death. Longline fishing by people who fish for sport also kills. Turtles become unintended catches instead of tuna or swordfish. Up to forty thousand turtles are killed every year by longline fishing. Earle believes that, as in all matters concerning the ocean and its creatures, when people are informed they can begin to care.

Amazing
Achievements

You have to love it before you are moved to save it.
—Sylvia Earle

Sylvia Earle's book *Sea Change* was successful in raising awareness and drawing people's attention to the many problems facing the ocean. Thousands of readers learned that the ocean is critical to their survival on earth. Earle was a celebrity who was known to be a spokesperson for the oceans.

In 1998, Earle's pleasure was visible when President Bill Clinton and Vice President Al Gore along with the United Nations (UN) declared the year to be the Year of the Ocean. Finally, Earle's hard work as ambassador of the oceans was being heard. Earle is passionate about everyone having an understanding of how critical the ocean is to each of us. This proclamation promoted public awareness and understanding of the importance and value of the ocean. It also made sure that the government would do all it could to promote exploring and wise use of its natural resources.

Later that year, Earle was praised by President Clinton for her work as the National Geographic Society's explorer-in-residence. He applauded her for her work with that organization and her work with the Sustainable Seas Expeditions.

The Sustainable Seas project was sponsored by the National Geographic Society and was led by Sylvia Earle. These expeditions of marine life made it possible for Earle and other scientists to explore the twelve protected marine sanctuaries in the United States. The scientists would use submersible technology like the Deep Rover subs designed by Earle and her former partner, Graham Hawkes. The mission would allow scientists to document the living history of each of the sanctuaries' plants and animals with photographs It would also provide schools with special programs on the importance of conservation and the importance of these sanctuaries.

Earle still makes presentations to school groups on the discoveries from this project. Thanks

Dr. Sylvia Earle, left, and an unidentified diver examine fish reference charts in the Florida Keys National Marine Sanctuary. On July 1, 1997, they launched the first day of the two-week Great American Fish Count, a coast-to-coast effort to document fish population, species' diversity trends, and bolster marine life awareness.

to Earle and Giddings's 1980 documentary on the whales in the Pacific, these creatures are making a comeback. Since 1966, they have been protected throughout their range. Many people have also discovered the whales' beautiful and haunting songs. Killer whales have respect now as well.

Because of her work, Earle was appointed the U.S. Deputy Commissioner to the International Whaling Commission. Earle was also the top adviser and producer of the 1977 film *Unforgettable Journey* produced by Giddings and whale scientist Roger Payne.

Even today, Earle has concerns about the whales. Their main food source is a thumb-size creature called krill. It is being harvested as food for cattle, poultry, and other livestock. This is because of krill's high protein content. Removing this small creature from the ocean means even seabirds have less to eat. Limits have been placed on krill harvesting in some areas, but they still become "bycatch" in the nets of today's fisherman. Earle says that "each species lost diminishes the chance that we [humans] can 'get it right.' . . . Every day, the number and demands of humankind increases; the size of the planet does not."[1]

In 1979, Earle's walk on the ocean floor in the Jim suit at a record-breaking depth of 1,250 feet gave her the title of "Her Deepness."

In the 1980s, her company shared with partner Hawkes, Deep Ocean Engineering, designed and built submersibles. This made it possible for scientists to explore depths in the ocean never before possible. Earle's company is run today by her daughter, Elizabeth Taylor, and is called DOER. This stands for Deep Ocean Exploration and Research. Earle is the chairman of the company. They continue to design, operate, support, and consult on manned robotic sub sea systems.

Earle's appointment by President George H. W. Bush in 1990 as chief scientist of National Oceanic and Atmospheric Administration (NOAA) gained Earle another title. She was often called "The Sturgeon General." Her two-year term helped make the organization's mission more like that of the National Aeronautics and Space Administration (NASA). She tried to make research an important goal of the organization. Her job as chief scientist allowed her to bring the environmental crisis of oil spills on those beaches involved to the attention of millions of citizens. During the period from 1991 to 1993, Earle provided an environmental study of the consequences of a despot's actions taken during the Gulf War. Her work both above and below the oceans was documented in a video for NOAA. In 1998, this organization awarded Earle with the United States Environmental Hero Award.

In 1998, *Time* magazine honored Earle for her many achievements as a scientist, explorer, author, lecturer, and environmentalist by naming her their first "Hero for the Planet." In the same year, she also received the Global 500 Environmental Award.

Earle's current record of more than seven thousand dives has allowed her to catalog the largest specimen sample from the ocean. She has discovered new species and plants and animals and, in her honor, new species have been named after her. For her historic dives, Earle has been honored and inducted into the National Woman's Hall of Fame and the International Scuba Hall of Fame. In 2000, Dr. Earle received the high honor of being named a Living Legend by the Library of Congress.

Earle's contributions do not just occur underwater. In addition to her first book, *Sea Change,* she has written books for young readers. Some of these titles include *Hello Fish* and *Sea Critters,* both published in 1999. In 2000, *Dive: My Adventures in the Deep Frontier* was published. Another of Earle's books takes readers on adventures to our national marine sanctuaries. *National Geographic's Atlas of the Ocean, the Deep Frontier* was written by Earle in 2001.

"Her Deepness," as Earle is called in a television commercial produced by the oil company

Kerr-McGee, believes in cooperation between business and science. Earle is on the board of directors of this huge corporation that drills for oil in the ocean. Kerr-McGee installed the world's first truss spar (a large cylinder-like platform that is very stable in deep water). This important use of deep-water technology is an environmentally friendly way to use the riches of the ocean for our energy needs today. Earle believes that knowledge is the greatest hope for the future when it comes to meeting environmental challenges: "The greatest threat to our world is ignorance."[2]

One of Earle's proudest and most hopeful moments came in 2006, when President Bush designated one hundred forty thousand square miles around the Hawaiian Islands a national monument. President Bush gave credit to Earle for educating him on the importance of this act. Within this newly protected area live more than seven thousand species of marine animals, 25 percent are found nowhere else on the earth. Some of these species are endangered, including fourteen hundred very endangered Hawaiian monk seals.

In 2008, Earle was honored for her lifetime of accomplishments and contributions to science. She was proud to have been named a Legend of the Sea. Earle's most recent contribution is in the development of submersibles. Her new company, Deep Search International, was developed in 2007.

Sylvia Earle with George W. Bush when Bush established the Northwestern Hawaiian Islands National Monument, 2006.

Hawaiian monk seal

The company's mission is to create awareness of the ocean's importance to all life, explore global waters, and inspire conservation action. Earle is the president of this company. Earle's company also hopes to launch a new Web-based ocean awareness campaign. Documentary filmmaking is

On Wednesday, August 1, 2007, Earle gave a speech to a Commonwealth Club gathering at San Francisco's Aquarium of the Bay.

another important way Deep Search International hopes to bring attention to the deep ocean. The company hopes to use funds for ocean exploration that adds to scientific knowledge and to further Earle's scientific works and writings.[3]

6

Knowledge Is Power

Many of us ask what can I, as one person, do, but history shows us that everything good and bad starts because somebody does something or does not do something.

—Sylvia Earle

Dr. Sylvia Earle stood on the sandy beach and gazed out into the blue-green water of her beloved Gulf of Mexico. She remembered fondly her great backyard in Clearwater. She remembered when it actually had clear water. "In the past few decades—my lifetime," Earle reflected, "the sea has changed; with each passing year, pressures on ocean resources and other resources increase, but the size of the ocean does not."[1] Earle knows history and the mistaken deeds of people cannot be changed. But, just as individual people can have a negative impact on nature, individuals can also have a very positive effect.

William Perrin was only one man. In the early 1970s, he became disturbed by the hundreds of thousands of dolphins being killed each year by U.S. tuna fishermen. The fishermen would surround a school of tuna with huge nets. They would then haul in their catch, and, in the process, hundreds of dolphins would be taken in the nets as well. This process killed many dolphins without a reason. Perrin tried to persuade the fishing industry that this was an unnecessary act. But he did not make any progress.

Not a person to give up, Perrin decided to ask the American consumer for help. Perrin educated Americans on the way many dolphins were killed so people could eat tuna. Many people decided he was right. These consumers stopped buying tuna until the fishing methods became "dolphin safe."

Some people may think they are not responsible for what happens to the ocean or its creatures. Some people think that because they do not ever visit the ocean or live near the ocean, they are not responsible. Everyone has a role to play. Everyone needs to care what happens to the ocean. Some of the reasons are:

⬆ On Tuesday, April 29, 2008, Chairman Edward Markey (D-Mass.) and the Select Committee on Energy Independence and Global Warming held a hearing to examine the impact global warming is having on the earth's oceans and ecosystems. Dr. Earle stands next to Chairman Markey who is on the far right.

*One-half of the U.S. population lives in a coastal area.

*One in every six jobs is somehow related to the ocean.

*One-third of the U.S. Gross National Product (the total value of goods and services produced during a certain time) is produced in a coastal area.[2]

Earle is not discouraged by the future. She knows the good news is that there is still time to change things. Each person makes choices every single day. Imagine what might happen if millions of people made the right choices every day. Earle believes everyone decides if he or she will throw trash in the garbage or in the ocean. People decide if they will make wise or poor food choices. Every day someone can decide to pick up that piece of junk or litter from the beach or leave it there.

Earle is encouraged about saving the coral reefs. Although more than one-fourth of the world's reefs have been destroyed, it is not too late to save the rest. Scientists believe the reefs can be saved if destructive practices are outlawed and pollution can be controlled. Citizens can help by:

*Spreading the word about the endangered reefs.

*Be an informed citizen. Do not buy objects taken from coral reefs.

⬆ Sylvia Earle cheers the new Google Earth 5.0 at the California Academy of Sciences in San Francisco. The new version of Google Earth includes, among other features, a three-dimensional map of the sea floor.

*Never pollute.

*Whenever possible, support conservation organizations.

*Write letters to elected officials such as your congressman or governor."[3]

As former chief scientist for NOAA, Earle knows how important letters are. Letters that are written by young people are very important. Letters from young people are read, passed around, and at times hung on bulletin boards. Lawmakers think it is great that young people care. Because they care, the people who make laws and policies think about the future these young people will have. They care about the world these young people will inherit.

In 2004, Earle appeared in the documentary film *The Last Journey for the Leatherback.* This largest species of sea turtle, along with others, is threatened by the current fishing methods used to catch swordfish and tuna. Fishermen set billions of baited longline hooks and miles of net. This method is the main reason for the sea turtles' decline.

We can all choose to make a difference to help protect the sea turtles. We can make wise choices when choosing seafood to eat. Educate yourself on the issues. Make sure that plastics are recycled properly. Sea turtles often think a piece of floating plastic is a jellyfish.

Earle believes communication is the missing link to understanding the problems in the ocean. Information can be shared with those who do not know about the concerns. She wants those who are informed to tell others how important the blue part of our planet is. She wants us to understand we are all connected to one another.

Earle thinks there should be great investments in exploration. It is her dream that our government and/or private organizations would invest as much in the exploration of the ocean as we have invested in outer space. Ninety-five percent of the ocean is unexplored. Earle knows that if we want to understand life on earth, it is important to understand life in the ocean.

Although Earle has spent many decades of her life devoted to preserving the ocean, she still has one dream that she hopes will come to pass. The deepest ocean trench is called the Mariana Trench. It lies two hundred ten miles from the coast of Guam in the Pacific Ocean. This trench is like a large cut in the ocean floor. It is 5,905 feet deeper than Mount Everest is tall. Only two people in the world have ever journeyed there. Earle would like to be the next person to make that undersea journey. She would make the dive in a small submersible.

Exploring the seas is critical to our future. Earle is persistent in her message that investment should be made to explore this great last frontier on our own planet. Scientists believe there could be more than 10 million undiscovered species in the ocean. Earle would love to be part of this discovery. Earle continues with fund-raising for her Ocean Everest project. This is the project to take scientists to the deepest part of the ocean. "We know more about Mars than we do about the oceans," Earle tells those who are willing to listen.[4] The oceans hold the answers to many mysteries of the history of life. The technology is available to take us down into the deep ocean. The ocean's best friend would like to see this happen in her lifetime.

Timeline

1935—Born Gibbstown, New Jersey on August 30.

1948—Family moves to Dunedin, Florida.

1955—Receives Bachelor of Science degree from Florida State University.

1956—Receives Masters degree in Botany from Duke University.

1964—Joins a National Science Foundation expedition in the Indian Ocean.

1966—Reveives Doctorate from Duke University

1970—Leads an all-female research expedition known as Tektite II, Mission 6 during which they lived underwater for two weeks.

1979—Make a solo dive to 1,250 feet beneath the surface without being connected to a support vessel.

1980—*Exploring the Deep Frontier* published.

1981—Cofounds a company called Deep Ocean Engineering.

1990—Accepts appointment as the Chief Scientist of the National Oceanic and Atmospheric Administration (NOAA).

1992—Founded Deep Ocean Exploration and Research to further advance marine engineering.

1995—*Sea Change: A Message From the Oceans* published.

1998—Named *Time* magazine's's first "hero of the planet" in 1998.

1998–2002—Named *National Geographic*'s Explorer in Residence. Leads the Sustainable Seas Expeditions, a five year program to the United States National Marine Sanctuary.

1999—*Wild Oceans: America's Parks Under the Sea* published.

2001—*The Atlas of the Ocean* published.

2009—Wins the TED Prize.

Glossary

advocate—Someone who works for a cause or in support of something.

algae—A large group of plantlike organisms, usually called seaweed.

alligator gar—A large species of freshwater fish in North America. The fish has two large rows of alligator-like teeth along with its snout, give it its name.

bioluminescence—The ability to give off light.

bycatch—Species unintentionally caught along with targeted species.

carbon monoxide—A colorless, odorless, and tasteless gas that is poisonous.

curator—A person in charge of a museum.

despot—An absolute ruler.

ecosystem—A unit in nature made up of all plants, animals, and microorganisms.

environmentalist—A person working to solve problems in the environment.

habitat—The region where a plant or animal usually lives.

mentor—A trusted friend, counselor, or teacher.

pneumonia—A serious inflammation of the lung.

porthole—A small circular window used on the hull of ships to let in light and air.

sanctuary—A place of protection.

specimen—A part or individual used as a sample of a whole.

Chapter Notes

Chapter 1. The Urge to Submerge

1. William Beebe, *Half Mile Down* (New York: Harcourt, Brace and Company), p. 10.

Chapter 2. A Scientist Is Born

1. "Sylvia Earle Interview: Undersea Explorer, January 27, 1991, Oakland, California,"

2. *Academy of Achievement, 2008* <http://www.achievement.org/autodoc/printmember/ear0int-1> September 9, 2007).

Chapter 3. "Her Deepness"

1. Sylvia A. Earle, *Sea Change: A Message of the Oceans* (New York: G.P. Putnam's Sons, 1995), p. 64.

2. Ibid., pp. 65–66.

3. Ibid. p. 66.

4. Ibid. p. 70.

5. Sylvia A. Earle, "The Gentle Whales," *National Geographic,* vol. 155, no. 1, January 1979, pp. 2,4.

6. "Sylvia Earle Interview: Undersea Explorer, January 27, 1991, Oakland, California," *Academy of Achievement,* 2008 <http://www.achievement.org/autodoc/printmember/ear0int-1> (November 24, 2008)

7. Sylvia Earle. "A Walk in the Deep," *National Geographic.* Vol. 157, no. 5. May 1980, p. 631.

8. Earle, Sylvia. *Sea Change: A Message of the Oceans.* (New York: G. P. Putnam's Songs, 1995) pp. 122–123.

Chapter 4. Oceans of Trouble

1. Elizabeth McGowan, "Trash Is Imperiling the Oceans," Waste News, June 25, 2007, vol. 13, Issue 4, p. 7, <http://www.accessmylibrary.com/coms2/summary_0286-31786585_ITM> (January 14, 2008).

2. Sylvia Earle. "Not Such A Fine Kettle of Fish," *Conservation International,* 2007, <http://web.conservation.org/exp/frontlines/people/06080501.xml> (September 20, 2007).

3. Robert Ovetz, Ph.D. "Sea Turtles: Ambassadors of the Ocean to Your Classroom," *Education Update Online,* August 2004, <http://www.educationupdate.com/archives/2004/september/html/spot-seaturtles.html> (February 8, 2008).

4. Douglas H. Chadwick, "Coral in Peril," *National Geographic,* vol. 195, no. 1, January 1999, p. 34.

5. Sylvia A. Earle, "Life Springs From Death in Truk Lagoon," *National Geographic,* vol. 149, no. 5, May 1976, p. 586.

6. Ibid.

7. Sylvia A. Earle, *Dive,* (New York: Scholastic, Inc., 1999), p. 24.

8. Kathleen Sullivan, "Documentary Shows Human Toll on Ancient Sea Turtles," *SFGate.com,* August 27, 2004, <http://www.sfgate.com/cgi-bin/article.cgi?file=c/a/2004/08/27/WBG0N8D7EV1.DTL> (February 8, 2008).

Chapter 5. Amazing Achievements

1. Sylvia A. Earle, *Sea Change: A Message of the Oceans* (New York: G.P. Putnam's Sons, 1995), p. 225.

2. Susan Eaton, "Explorer Feels at Home in the Deep," *Deep Sea Explorer,* <http://www.aapg.org/explorer/2003/04apr/earle.cfm> (January 22, 2008).

3. Deep Search International, "Welcome to Deep Search International," <http://deepsearch.org/index.html> (February 29, 2008).

Chapter 6. Knowledge Is Power

1. Sylvia A. Earle, *Sea Change: A Message of the Oceans* (New York: G.P. Putnam's Sons, 1995), pp. 322–323.

2. Dr. Mark Hixon, *Ten Things YOU Can Do to Save Our Ocean!* <http://dusk2.geo.orst.edu/oceans/yoto.html> (May 5, 2008).

3. Ibid.

4. Michael D. Lemonick, "The Last Frontier," *Time,* August 14, 1995, <http://www.time.com/time/printout/0,8816,983295,00.html> (March 23, 2008).

Further Reading

Books

Baker, Beth. *Sylvia Earle, Guardian of the Sea* Minneapolis: Lerner Publications, 2001

Cullen, Katherine. *Marine Science: The People Behind the Science.* New York: Chelsea House, 2006.

Hitchcock, Susan Tyler. *Sylvia Earle: Deep-Sea Explorer.* Philadelphia: Chelsea House, 2004.

Internet Addresses

Sylvia Earle Profile – Academy of Achievement
<www.achievement.org/autodoc/page/ear0pro-1>

Sylvia Earle—Oceanographer
Get information, facts, and more about world-renowned oceanographer Sylvia Earle from *National Geographic.*
<www.nationalgeographic.com/field/explorers/sylvia-earle.html>

Books by Sylvia Earle

Earle, Sylvia A., and Linda K. Glover. *Ocean: An Illustrated Atlas*. Washington, D.C.: National Geographic Society, 2008.

Earle, Sylvia A., and Henry Wolcott. *Wild Ocean: America's Parks Under the Sea*. Washington, D.C.: National Geographic Society , 1999.

Earle, Sylvia A. *Sea Change: A Message from the Oceans*. New York: Ballantine Books, 1999.

Earle, Sylvia A. *The Call of the Sea*. Washington, D.C.: National Geographic Society, 1978.

For younger readers:

Earle, Sylvia A. *Hello Fish!: Visiting the Coral Reef.* Washington, D.C.: National Geographic Children's Books, 2001.

Earle, Sylvia A. *Jump into Science: Coral Reefs*. Washington, D.C.: National Geographic Children's Books, 2003.

Earle, Sylvia A. *Sea Critters*. Washington, D.C.: National Geographic Children's Books, 2006.

Earle, Sylvia A. *Dive!: My Adventures in the Deep Frontier.* Washington, D.C.: National Geographic Children's Books, 1999.

Index

DATE DUE